WHEN AFRICAN-AMERICANS STOP THE VIOLENCE: HALLELUJAH!

C. SAMUEL JOHNSON, II

authorHOUSE®

AuthorHouse™
1663 Liberty Drive
Bloomington, IN 47403
www.authorhouse.com
Phone: 1 (800) 839-8640

Published by AuthorHouse 08/24/2017

ISBN: 978-1-5246-9816-4 (sc)
ISBN: 978-1-5246-9814-0 (hc)
ISBN: 978-1-5246-9815-7 (e)

Library of Congress Control Number: 2017910109

Print information available on the last page.

CONTENTS

ACKNOWLEDGMENTS

This is my second book. The first, *The Journey of A Common Man: Perceptions, and Reflections.* It consisted of memoirs, and a collection of stories and personal situations, whereas, my life had been guided by and situated with our Maker and Creator as the chief architect. Yes, the summary cited certain vital and crucial events that happened over time in my life which caused a realization, understanding and the importance of trusting God in all endeavors.

I cited particular gratitude to my mother and father, who have been with God for many years, but they were on earth long enough for me to appreciate and cherish their existence, assistance to me, and everything on my behalf. One of my brothers was more of an inspirational leader in my life, until his death at a very young age. It would be inappropriate for me not to mention my sisters, and their family members, for the immense support and understanding during the writing and editing of my previously stated book. But without the inspiration of the Lord, and his divine guidance and wisdom, none of this would have been possible.

I cite the following individuals for their assistance regarding this book. The names alphabetically are: Dr. A. R. Towns--Author, Editor and Medical Consultant; Ms. Sherrie A. Williams—Early Childhood Development & Consultant; Ms. Yolanda R. Williams –Director/Teaching Artist; Yvetta L. Williams—Kai Productions/Reel Walk Cinema, L.L.C.; and Ms. Yvonne C. Williams, Writer/Editor. This brief book focuses on my impressions, observations, and history of life, research, race and living in America, 2016-17, as an African -American. It also explores the various twists and turns required for existing without becoming a casualty, resulting from living the so-called average number of years. Furthermore, this summary cites various solutions to many of life's challenges in the 21st century, with the most important one, "showing personal faith in God."

INTRODUCTION

I t appears that a significant percentage of the nation's population has become "materialistic" driven. Those "with," seem to have begun alienating themselves from those "without." People working in service jobs are increasing, while professional opportunities tend to be in short supply. Conversely, it is not that people can't perform in those kinds of jobs, but the numbers are not available for the ones seeking professional positions. Thus, begins a trend of underemployment, with people accepting service job positions. The effects of the local and national media have further enhanced how people view worldly items and what it takes to secure those articles of value. Further, the minimum wage factor also tends to influence the outcome of what individuals can acquire and how they can be secured. The drive toward money continues to escalate. A large number of African-Americans and other minorities in the job-seeking-age category have increased. But in America, there will continue to be somewhat high unemployment rates, dependent upon the section one resides. However, according to a report I saw on the local news (Jan. 2017), the range is approximately 4 to 5 percent. That is dependent on the socio-economic status and the life style of the individuals. I will also examine the intricacies that may reflect a so-called "cause and affect," situation among African-Americans in America.

Well, why don't people choose areas that would satisfy employers who are looking for workers? One reason is that not all people possess the kind of intellectual capacities to perform in certain jobs, thus, leaving companies seeking those who possess skills they want. That is one factor that makes the employment picture complicated. America is not a country that is communistic in values, where, if there are not enough people for a particular company, and individuals do not desire to work at the company, they would be forced to do so, or jailed, killed or some other ill-fated consequence. Sorry, this is America, so-called home of the brave, and land of the free. That is the motto or story often given this country. Those individuals, who have secured the adequate education, and training or skill, may be able to secure positions in the labor force, which are paid substantial dollars for their services. Those without, may not be so fortunate.

Readers, my writings will take various twists and turns, while trying to remain focused on the plight of young African-Americans, and other minorities in the 21st century. I will also cite the effects of religion as it relates to the same group, and their continued struggles in America. I will examine racism, as it affects the racial climate, and how the dominant race reacts when human rights are involved. Further, why do African-Americans continue to execute violent crimes toward each other, far more than any other race in America? That question remains open for debate and discussion in the 21st century. Another issue for discussion will be how the "haves" versus the "have-nots," continue to be of significant concern for African-Americans and all Americans. And finally, when will they (African-Americans) understand, and begin to show "true love" for each other, regarding personal rights, and responsibilities associated with day-to-day living? I have not investigated each entity in-depth because such an endeavor would require that readers scan more and more pages than actually reading them. The number of pages in this book would certainly increase, thus jeopardizing the book's integrity, which cannot happen. Readers, be advised that my usage of the terms "African-Americans" or "blacks" and "dominant race," or "white," in this book, are interchangeable and or the same.

CHAPTER ONE

UNDERSTANDING YOUR LIFE

W ell, I will begin with the first concern, that of self, or personal rights and responsibilities regarding others, and particularly other African-Americans. Readers, yes it is hard living in America and is becoming more and more difficult each passing year. Allow me to deviate a moment as I inject a few news reports. It is hard living in certain parts of America, very, very hard. That situation is easily traced to their heritage as African-Americans. However, there is one common denominator about that status in this country. Truthfully, most African-Americans are considered to be less respected than the dominant race (white). This book, in contrast to the excellent one written by Kelly Brown Douglas (2015), titled, *"Stand Your Ground: Black Bodies and the Justice of God,"* is an attempt to provide personal in-depth views regarding

1

African-Americans and the divisiveness that rests therein. I also explore how the so-called "have-nots" often dominate the overall banal label applied to all African-Americans. But there are exceptions to their concept that most of us are non-productive, and not working. In actuality, that group only applies to less than 10 percent!

Historically, we have always been the so-called, second class citizens because of laws, rules, regulations and overall prejudiced views promoted by the dominant race. Hundreds of years have passed since African-Americans arrived in America. But, has the race decided to quit the fight for equality? No, I don't think so! If the community would only surmise, if possible, how conditions were hundreds of years ago, probably a rude awakening would happen. We are alive in the 21st century because of the diligence and perseverance our fathers and mothers executed years and years in the past. Yes, killings took place, but most were master-slaves precipitated, and on occasions, there were slaves killing slaves. But because they were considered to be valuable properties, belonging to the masters, it was not encouraged.

In the perils of bondage African-Americans continued year-after-year with few reasons to express hope in their lives, but in spite of their dire conditions, most did not want to die. Even with hardships, trials, tribulations, and often promises of permanent slavery, they managed to maintain the desire to live, if for no other reason than the sake of their children. In addition, they were not considered American citizens. But they had hopes that many situations would significantly improve in later years.

"Christ will make his home in our hearts, through faith."

Ephesians 3-17 (REV)

It is almost impossible for the 21st century African-Americans to imagine those years and the kind of conditions, but there are museums and books, including media shows to remind them of those slavery conditions. This served to further verify that the suffering and hardship did exist. The elderly and their ancestors, were they alive, could provide a significant amount of information about those yesteryears.

I took the liberty to cite the prior because African-Americans need to become wiser and understand what it meant to be a slave. The current challenges are for them to reconcile the results and affects that it had on their present-day situations, if any. But can there be a correlation between what happened years and years in the past to what is transpiring in today's world regarding violence? That is a very difficult question to answer without adequate research pertaining thereto. What is happening in America, in the form of violence, is often the wrong way to achieve most positive results. Killings of innocent victims cannot and will not do anything to alter the affects slavery had on them. Further, what caused societal changes in the way African-Americans were treated and viewed by the dominant race was carefully crafted by men and women of distinction, who cared about what was to happen in the future toward the same. There were early heroes, that included people, if memory serves me correctly, as George Washington Carver, Malcolm X, Booker T. Washington, Mary M. Bethune, Daniel Payne and Dorothy Height, to name a few. African-Americans, in the 21st century, tend to act as if those heroes of yesteryears labored in vain. They suffered and endured all kinds of humiliation so those that followed, would, and could be free to pursue life, liberty, the pursuit of happiness, and insure domestic tranquility; something that they never had, as stated in the constitution. Yes, I did use that kind of a quote when referencing "violence and African-Americans." Why destroy the past that was begun and built by others of similar color, who exhibited strength, and wisdom, and compassion for each other and those that followed? Do they not cherish life anymore? What about the lives of others? Everyone has the right to live and prosper, do they not? Do they have the authority and infinite power to take away the life of another regardless of the reason(s)? The chances are high that the existence of the person committing the violence is or will be doomed, along with the person killed. Such a tragedy! Who wins? Well, readers, there is no winner. There is not an individual on earth with the power to restore life, the next day, year, or ever again. We will never see them again. Why execute hardship, drama, sadness and grief for the families involved?

Yes, those yesteryears of slavery did have a significant influence on their lives. Today, the residual effects continue in some regards. Are they pleased with themselves? No! The stain of slavery remains in many regards. For example, the prosperity that the dominant class has versus those that are attributed to African-Americans is unmistakable, and can be attributed to slavery. Okay, there are many reasons that may justify the results, but this is not the chapter to discuss those issues. Later chapters will expound on some in some detail. Therefore, one may not have the riches of this world, but are African-Americans alive? Yes. Starving? No. Yes, all would like something better, but the dominant race had those restrictions in place long before African-Americans were so-called free, and unfortunately, the masses have chosen not to destroy their systems. That ensures a continuation of the same! The dominant race tends to be the "haves." But African-Americans should not allow them to dictate a feeling of subjugated thoughts about themselves. The systems have always been uneven, and the same is true today. But to allow the dominant race continued domain over their thoughts, feelings, and actions, should not continue to exist. Whatever course of action is necessary, should be investigated. They should decide what to do and have a plan of action to achieve whatever goals are set. Deciding the kind of representation in the form of individuals would show society that they are serious about overcoming the many vestiges that slavery has left. They need African-Americans who have worked to achieve greatness and are continuing to aspire, motivate and encourage each other to do the same. That does not mean exhibiting violent behaviors toward each other and society. The law-abiding African-Americans should be leading the parades for justice. They cannot expect alleged or convicted felons or those in illegal activities to carry the torch of democracy for the law- and-order African-Americans. That seems to be a pattern in the 21st century. They cannot get justice with so-called criminals leading the way! Sorry, but that is my contention. Those individuals are already jail-bound or recently released from prison. Furthermore, given a chance, you will become their next victim either via robberies, killings, assaults, etc. African-Americans should show some pride and dignity in pursuing their cause for freedom. Do not allow the dominant race to say who and where you are going regarding self-prosperity, other than higher and higher.

Now, the following discussion is somewhat sad for me to cite. That is, African-Americans self-destruction of each other, males, females, the elderly and children. Can we say that their attitudes toward violence and crime are the result of what the dominant race has managed to foster toward them over the years? Well, I will attempt to investigate those assumptions. I have read many books and or articles regarding their communities and the attempt to justify living, and particularly as it relates to a theological concept. It would not be proper if the mention of religion and African-Americans were not intertwined. In addition, the contemporary dominant race (Caucasian) issues continue to manifest themselves, and their views on critical issues dealing with race, and the African-Americans status in America. Has God forsaken them, or was He not there from the beginning? Those are vital issues that will lead into the next chapter.

CHAPTER TWO

CRITICAL ISSUES FOR AFRICAN-AMERICAN MEN AND WOMEN: FAITH AND RACISM

"Faith"

I will make a brief attempt to address the faith and racism issues in this chapter. Please pardon me, as the readers are about to be reintroduced to a historical version of African-Americans belief system and how it is directly related to their faith in God. From that perspective, most of their religious teachings were biblically conveyed by the dominant race (Caucasians) at that time. Those kinds of instructions were time sensitive, encompassing hundreds of years before the 21st century. Most individuals in America were then, and are now Christians, and most utilized the Christian

Bible (King James Version). King James was available to employ others, scribes, scholars, etc., to translate the Bible. But who took credit in the form of a name affixed to the Bible? Yes, you guessed, King James. Furthermore, the Bible, which is composed of scriptures, was to have been inspired by God, through visions, spiritual utterances, etc. Now, most have heard that it was written by God and full of his utterances. Only a person with limited understanding would conclude that God wrote everything in the King James Version of The Holy Bible!

Having read a significant portion of the life and works of King James has created an ongoing inquiry into the kinds of biblical translations and thoughts used. According to Fraser (1994), he was quite emotionally disturbed during his formative years. In 1589, he crossed the seas from Norway to secure Anne of Denmark to be his wife. The marriage began well, according to Fraser (1994), and produced several children, of which two were sons, Henry, Charles, and a daughter Elizabeth. Before this writing, I was aware that there was a difference in being inspired by the Holy Spirit (God), and being a King, appointed at birth. Therefore, how could the revisions or translations is attributed to the Holy Father? While reading the information purported by Fraser (1994), in The

Court and Character of King James, it showed that he oversaw the translation of the King James Bible. Kind of interesting readers! What do you think about my research on the prior?

Well, I have presented a brief summary of King James, who is reported responsible for getting the Bible translated. There are many other translations, but this one was adapted by Christians in America for usage. It may be difficult for many African-American Christians to believe some of their translations. Many tend to think that valuable texts are missing. Purposely? If so, why?

"Racism"

Now, I will return to African-Americans and their concern for religious thinking and the acceptance of God in their lives. From the time they arrived in the New World, religion was an important part of their lives. They brought aspects of religion with them and their so-called masters could not and did not understand. In later years, after they had assimilated the slaves into their way of thinking, and so-called culture, some slaves were allowed to explain to the masters their meanings, and what was going on when they were celebrating, and dancing. Once the masters felt comfortable and had a reasonable understanding of what they were doing, many were taught a different language, and with it came their representation of God. Many hundreds of years have passed, and now, African-Americans have, and are aware of several Gods, from Jesus to Buddha. The worship of various Gods has always been known. The slaves with their Gods from their country and the dominant race (white) with their God. These are also apparent in that African-Americans (now), but slaves (hundreds of years ago), were separate and not equal. This practice has continued for hundreds of years and is omnipresent today.

It has been my view for many years that racism is what should be called, "learned behavior." Babies are not born with knowledge of who they are and from whence they came. Therefore, for them to develop from infancy to adulthood, most knowledge must be learned. What kind of teaching and by who often determines, to a great deal, what happens and the kind of thought processes are present. Therefore, my contention is that most, if not all, can be called prejudiced. How? Numerous environmental factors can influence overall attitudes. For example, African-Americans may tend to be prejudiced toward one or several racial groups. Why is it often a convoluted rationale? They may not like certain behaviors often associated with Mexicans people, who in term, may not like Caucasians, for whatever reasons exist. Furthermore, the Japanese may not like Chinese, and others, for whatever the reasons associated in addition to that. In essence, we are all prejudice to various degrees. For a moment, I will take a closer look at racism and see what the Merriam-Webster Dictionary (2016), has to say regarding a definition of the term. As a noun, racism is defined as "hatred or intolerance by another race or other races," or "the belief that some races are inherently superior (physically, intellectually, or culturally) to others, and they have a right to dominate them." How to change racial patterns of the different ethnic groups is an incredibly complex task. Individual ethnicity groups, in the 21st century, have begun to engage in group sessions of diversity people meetings, to bring forth dialogue for easing and understanding each other in America. Mind you, eradication of racism is not going to happen overnight, but little by little, progress can be made toward, hopefully, removing hatred and other stigmas associated thereto.

It is often evident here in America that racism, particularly by whites against blacks, has created profound racial tension and conflict in virtually all aspects of American society. It wasn't until the civil rights movement of the 1950s and 1960s that some vestiges of white domination over blacks were removed. However, it was not supported by all branches and levels of government. "Denying Blacks their civil rights and opportunities to participate in political, economic, and social communities became a definite struggle for them and other minorities."(U.S. Census Bureau, 201, 2010).

In the 21st century, although it has never gone away, the old evil phrase has risen again in various areas of our society. That phrase would be, "whatever the master says is right." Of course, that can be viewed in many different ways. However, my concern deals primarily with many "law enforcement" practices of the men and women sworn to "protect and serve." I will not cite the already known racial incidents that have occurred throughout various communities, thereby, gaining attention locally and eventually nationally, in this country. The racial complexities that have become important in the lives of Americans cannot be resolved by enacting a policy or laws to prevent such atrocities of one group toward another, regardless of the ethnicities involved. I have seen and experienced situations that would cause serious problems for young African-Americans. For example, the thought of having been turned away by the dominant race for wanting and deciding to sit at lunch counters. In many instances, the same law enforcement personnel, sworn to "protect and serve," were responsible for the abusiveness that happened. Mind you, there were laws and policies to protect them in

He that hath mercy on the poor happy is he.

Proverbs (14:21) (KJV)

their endeavors, against what I will now label as "minorities." Yes, blacks were fortunate to have any rights, compared to those of the dominant race (Caucasian). How did they survive those kinds of discriminative actions? The times before my birth are defined through emotional accounts, as being worse. Imagine how my father, mother, grandfather, grandmother, etc., managed to survive through the worse conditions of discrimination that were possible? Further, compared to situations in the 21st century, involving minorities and law enforcement personnel, with those of past decades, they would be unmentionable.

Yes, times have certainly changed for the better. But listening to the current media regarding individual events of law enforcement personnel and their relationship with African-Americans and other minorities, one would think that they were living in those turbulent unchangeable times of the past one hundred years.

Hello America, times have changed, and it is important that all Americans, regardless of their status, understand each other. As previously mentioned, we also must not continue allowing those individuals who have been convicted of crimes, or known felons marching in black lives matter demonstrations, to foster the burden of conflict and attention to problems that may affect the overall population of blacks and other minorities. In contrast, long ago; okay, many of my readers do not want to hear about the past and "those old days." Leaders of marches and demonstrations staged by African-Americans for their rights were lead by civil rights leaders of distinction. For example, the Dr. M. L. King, Jr., Minister Louis Farrakhan, Rev. Jesse Jackson, and Dr. Ralph Abernathy. Yes, these men were known as fighters for civil rights of African-Americans and other minorities in America. Yes, their times have come and gone. The new leaders of the Urban league, NAACP, etc., have been elected to bear the torch for freedom, but what are they doing or have done regarding the movement to foster right from wrong? Can you name someone who is leading the so-called movement today, the 21st century, male or female? Mind you, the struggles were different then, than they are today. I would imagine that a new kind of strategy would be needed for the struggles during the 21st century. Do African-Americans think the movement is all over, and justice and equality mixed with the abolishment of racisms, has been achieved? I think not! Yes, I made the statement that many of the same feel my prior statements are true, and it is all over, and living in paradise has happened! But to be honest, the majority of African-Americans living in America has increased their materialistic incomes to a very high percentage compared to those of the 1960s and 1970s. As I stated in the prior sentences, it is a new and different kind of struggle that deals with intrinsic values versus that which is not, and known as extrinsic values. They are what most African-Americans would consider as "living well." What that means is for the reader to interpret. What can be done to solidify the movements, and struggles encountered by them and other minorities in America? Those questions, along with others, have been asked by people of importance and the general population for years. The resolutions are few that would resolve the problems on a permanent basis. Had I the skill, and knowledge that would solve these problems, and use preventative measures, which would guarantee that they would not resurface in the future; this author would be in demand as a billion dollar speaker!

Readers, I have read many articles, books and historical treatises regarding the problems and issues of racism and how to treat those kinds of behaviors. But, most suggestions and considerations have not worked. I would propose the somewhat controversial recommendation (AI), to some degree, for what may or may not resolve many of the problems dealing with racism. First, I must define what is meant by the term, and how it would introduce a new solution to the ongoing current racism situation in America. Recently, I viewed a documentary on television involving the concept of Artificial Intelligence. In essence, machines would propose solutions to problems based on the facts, and make intelligent decisions free of the emotionalism that are exhibited by humans. Will the measures be implemented or addressed? It is hard to make a determination at this time. However, I conclude that over time, those and other answers will be addressed and unique solutions made.

The African-Americans must have a mandate for those in power to utilize. The same old course of actions that continue will not cause problems to be solved. That would require work in a timely and efficient manner, especially with the same kind of tools previously used. It is a simple reaction to situations that occur at a given point in time. African-Americans must continue striving to help resolve their own problems with education, motivation, and not violence. As I have stated in prior paragraphs, there are individuals who have lead the way to improving self and the race as a whole. They continue to perform, even in the 21st century. I would like to introduce readers to similar information written by a contemporary and famous African-American female named Ms. Oprah Winfrey. Her latest book is titled: *The Life You Want.* In it, she shares many, many experiences, both good and bad, with hopes to inspire, encourage and motivate others to explore life to the fullest. Okay, you may not want to hear what she has written during the 21st century. But I have comments to those who share such criticism, "where is your empire worth over two billion dollars?" Through hard work, perseverance, and genius, she has become the only female African-American billionaire in America, and most respected celebrity in the world. No, she did not get it on "easy street." In contrast, she worked, and worked and worked again. She failed many, many times, but continued to get up, always to where she is today. Does it matter whether she is an African-American woman and not a man? I think not! In her words, "I know for sure that healing the wounds of the past is one of the biggest and most worthwhile challenges of life." (Winfrey) 2017. Well, that is also part of the problem for many American-Americans, "not acknowledging worth-while successes;" not those of sports, movies, music, etc., but those tangibles where all can strive to become and succeed overtime. Now I ask, can the wounds of "slavery-past" be healed by African-Americans overtime?

CHAPTER THREE

WHY ARE AFRICAN-AMERICANS KILLING EACH OTHER, IF BLACK LIVES MATTER?

Readers, it is unusual for me to write this book using free expressions, thoughts, and reflections, on situations, directly or indirectly affecting the lives of African-Americans. No, they were not newly arrivals in this country. Slaves were first brought to the new world from Africa centuries ago. However, if an individual would cogitate about the current state of affairs in this country, one would think that the so-called slave trades were back in business and that African-Americans were being used and killed by the dominant race. But, no, that is not happening. There are "killings," but most have been toward each other. Not to imply that there were fewer murders in the past, but the broadcast media

firstly, but not necessarily in order of rationale, are in competition

with other communications for ratings; which increase dollars and

cents. Mind you, I am not implying that they are responsible for

the killings by African-Americans against each other. Secondly,

individuals seek and get attention for violence, so why would people

risk their lives but for the obvious reason of getting attention? Most

or many of those getting arrested or stopped by law enforcement

personnel are alleged and or convicted felons, have outstanding

police warrants, traffic violations, or have committed crimes. And

thirdly, the automobile driven, in many instances, tends to have a

moving violation pending. And for the law enforcement personnel

to detain and stop the vehicle for notification of the same, and

provide means for corrective actions, is often a necessary objective.

In fairness to everyone, some law enforcement stops are pure and

simply "racial" in nature. That should serve as a reminder for those

stopped, to try and obey the officer's command in the best manner

possible. Do not give him or her pleasure of attempting to commit

a crime toward you, the driver. That is fine and dandy Mr. Author,

but why are they shooting the individuals when the vehicle is

stopped? Excellent question and my answer may surprise most

readers. For a moment, place yourself in the position of an officer or law enforcement personnel. That is, stopping an automobile without a partner in your car. Suppose the vehicle stopped has a missing tail light, and the stop was only to advise the driver of the same, and maybe, provide him or her with a written reminder to make the corrections promptly. It could be that the next officer who stops the vehicle may not be in a forgiving mood. However, the person driving the vehicle is wanted on an outstanding warrant and decides to outrun the patrol car. Does the officer know this? No! Now, the chase begins, and once the vehicle has stopped and the driver is asked to step out of the car, hands in the air, etc., the officer performs other administrative duties.

God is always there to lead and guide.

The driver decides not to step out, and another chase begins, only to finally be apprehended with street spikes, blowing out the tires. The driver is again asked to get out of the car with hands up. If the driver tries any motions after being invited to step out of the car with hands up, or in the air, shooting may pursue. Or, if the driver decides to disobey all of the law enforcement directives, what is the officer to do? In many cases, who knows what could follow. Suppose a white officer fatally shoots a black male who somehow pulls a weapon and fires, missing the officer. Now, what is the officer to do? National attention is often given to those kinds of incidents without knowing all of the facts and circumstances. Yes, many news sites are quick to bring forth drama, which most of the time promotes citizens anger toward the officers. I am aware that many African-Americans are shot on a weekly or daily basis in the city of Chicago, IL. Is that not the place where the former President, Mr. Obama, claimed temporary non-white house residence? If memory serves me correctly, he mentioned those killings only a few times during his eight years as President. Many of those killings involved innocent victims (juveniles, young children, women, and bystanders) in crowds. Why do those incidents tend to attract limited national attention and media coverage? Well, one reason could be that they continue to involve violence of blacks killing each other, and not whites! I may not agree with that statement, but it is true. I wonder what the results would be if the opposite was true, and more whites are being killed by blacks, in the central metropolitan cities of America? Did I make my obvious thoughts known? I think so!

We, as people, should admonish all violence in this country, and that certainly includes the taking of lives. The Federal Government should also provide some attention to those kinds of problems in particular states, whether assistance is requested or not! How can we honestly speak about the wars in Syria, Iraq, Afghanistan and other world countries, when we cannot or choose not to control the violence in this country?

I recently read an article printed July 29, 2012, by the Associated Press, and published in the Clarion Ledger, Jackson, MS paper titled: "Barrack Obama Era:" About his refusal to specially target any programs dealing with high school unemployment among African Americans, An interviewer from Black Entertainment Television asked Mr. Obama, "Why Not?" he replied, "That's not how America Works?" Well, well Sir, my questions to you Mr. President are, "How does America work?" and "Does it work?" By his administration giving the entire stimulus monies to the co-called "Big Shots" of Wall Street? Did his actions allow them to provide millions of dollars to their people in the form of bonuses, when the rest of Americans went hurting because of the monies being so-called lost?

I was appalled at the answer given by the President, and equally shocked that African-Americans did not make significant efforts to request demands from him, which he may have addressed immediately; then, maybe not! In contrast, another President in history has done so. If memory serves me accurately, President Lyndon Johnson of Texas, a southern Democrat, during the sixties and Kennedy administration, came to mind. I will make reference to the specified programs he provided in a later chapter. But that response was not what a commoner would have expected from a President of America.

Your answer should have reflected more definitive kind of a response, especially from someone of your authority. Yes, I realize that you were the President and the answers to important questions are made, especially by the President of the United States of America. Perhaps, the newly elected President, Mr. D. Trump, will find time to give attention to those three or four items that he cited during his campaign regarding the status of African-American communities, which included high unemployment, crime, and dilapidated communities. Good Luck!

Those were simply the views of this ordinary, but educated man, as of February 10, 2017. Have they changed as I write May 10, 2017? I think not! The former President did not in eight years, regardless of whether congress or the senate approved his initiatives, address those kinds of problems or situations in the African-American communities. Could he have signed Executive Orders, as Mr. Trump has done in the short time he has been President more than any other in the history of Presidents? I think so! In summary, conditions in the inner cities of this country are deplorable, crime is out of control, the infrastructure continues to crumble; the instructional school systems in many major urban cities are substandard or inadequate, and easily comparable to a third-world country. What can be done, by whom, and how long will it take for a revitalization to begin and end? No one seems to care as long as they are in their houses away from the entire previously described situations. Moreover, we are talking about many middle-class families who are also afraid to leave their homes for fear of break-ins; and the children cannot play outside because of the same, "crime and gunfire."

Ladies and gentlemen, we are constantly facing the future generation with hope, but also unknown questions and answers. For example, those living in an upper-class white neighborhood would not subscribe to those kinds of thoughts (nightly gun-fire in the neighborhood), as being common every day events. Why? They are not with those kinds of people in their neighborhoods and surroundings. However, the only realizations many encounter are nightly or world news with viewpoints and other events captured in particular crime- ridden areas, where it is not surprising to see and experience those events many times a year.

What tends to generate more and more crime in neighborhoods and other areas in cities is something simply, and that is transportation. It has become a necessity in the 21st century, and has also become an easy means to commit crimes in heretofore remote areas. We see the trend particularly if the target crime area is near a major interstate. Yes, most businesses and large establishments have cameras and other preventative crime devices, whereas those who commit offenses can quickly be identified and apprehended. However, are those measures enough to prevent crimes? I think not! Although there is a certain degree of sophistication used in trying to prevent crimes, those committing the offenses tend to stay one-step ahead of law-enforcement. I often think why is it that those so-called black leaders do not march and bring forth national exposure or attention when they (other blacks) continue to kill each other daily? Okay, that statement seems to be mentioned in this book more than other items. A true fact, but it should be cited until the violence stops! Those drive-bys tend to kill innocent people, especially children, and females. Most of those kinds of killings are drug-related. Yes, they also tend to involve domestic altercations; and those protesters have the audacity to shout, "Black Lives Matter!" Hello protestors. Is that a correct statement? Yes or no? African-Americans kill each other daily, and often law enforcement turns the other way or away from the crime because their views are, "Another one dead," and "Probably a trouble-maker or Convicted or accused felon with a record or warrant." "Therefore, our jobs are easier, because he or she is off the streets and cannot harm anyone again." Now, I ask the question: Black lives matter to whom? Surely, not to the many blacks who continue to kill the same on a daily basis! We need to face the facts boys and girls. Many African-Americans are now using drugs and other narcotics, and even the new fad (my references) called (opioids) drugs. My contention is that if you deal with drugs long enough, either the dealers will destroy you, or the narcotics will do the job. Very few users make a complete separation from those situations and live freely and healthy again. It rarely happens in the 21st century. Yes, there are treatment centers, and they are supposed to help and provide treatment for an eventual cure. But who has the monies for those kinds of actions? Now, can we blame the politicians, who tend to turn deaf ears to the situations? I think not! There are hundreds of other issues in the U. S. that command their attention and focus. But crimes and drugs in the inner cities are not included. However, if it affected their lives, businesses, children, and women, they would become interested. Only tragic! When will African-Americans begin to think similarly? What could change the climate and make drugs become an addiction of the past?

I have seen throughout many years of existence, which numbers over seventy, a gradual, but consistent move away from the teachings of God. My question is, can God be the answer? Historically, African-American communities have been grounded in teachings of God, via biblical scriptures and reinforced by families. It appears that a significant segment of the younger generation have moved away from or steered from God and His teachings. They seem not to have any feelings for a person's life. Killing tends to be the norm for that segment of the African-American population. A result, "the criminal justice system" becomes an entire lifetime place of resident. Tragic! Why? Do they not attend church anymore? Their elders and grandparents did and made efforts to instill the same Godly doctrine in their lives. But many statistics show it has not worked or has failed. I only ask the question as, "Do they think that God is real?" "Do they trust or have faith in God?"

I recall a biblical story told by the late minister, Rev. C. L. Franklin of Detroit, MI. He was delivering a sermon about Moses and his deeds, dealing with the people. While leading them to the purported Promised Land from Egypt, the minister said, "In the beginning, God created man in his image; and man reversed the tables, thus trying to create God in his image." They were making statues of Him, in bronze, symbols of animals, etc., and gold, that would represent God. Something the people could or would see, and not believe in the invisible God that Mosses was proclaiming. No, many people of the so-called gospel do not portray a bright and holy image that many black youths can follow the example of Him, and his marvelous works. I often think of the situation in several churches and with Christians in America. Yes, they want to reduce God to whatever image and or category possible, and use Him at their disposal. For example, readers have heard in many churches, proclaimed by a minister of the so-called gospel, that, "God told me if you did not properly submit a seed, some kind of evil or accident would happen to you." Hello readers, nothing is more from the truth. That saying is appropriately called, according to the Merriam-Webster Dictionary (2016), "anthropomorphic," a "humanistic kind of projection." "Trying to humanize, simply, an attempt to lower the size of being," and changing, "God into a human type of mortal." That is simply an atrocity! I will not surmise that most African-Americans give thought to that sort of thinking, but many do not attend Church and don't believe in God, until it is time to, as I call I it, "come on home," or "die."

What have they learned that inspire them to kill their own more than the dominant race or any other group? As I referenced in my prior book, only "the lack of love for oneself." If one does not love himself or herself, how does one understand or know how to love another? (Not love as a boy would love a girl). For a large number of them, the 21st century has brought forth many sounding more and more like the biblical version of Moses, and his episodes, while trying to lead the children out of Egypt to the Promised Land. God today, seems to be so-called green (money), and other items of personal value. For example, diamond, silver, gold, cooper, etc. It is good that God does not take immediate actions against us for the many misdeeds made against Him, and mistruths postulated today against the same. The necessity of possessing material values in our society has created an epidemic. The "haves" tend to increase their wealth, while the "have-nots" do not have capital to grow at all. Could it be that the many African-American youths of today see their fate as useless, and do not care; because who cares about them? Are we watching a total vanishing of those without a reason to live amongst each other in our society of material surpluses? What must be done to change the culture of African-Americans in our society? Can they continue to count on those "marches" in order to secure justice and equality? Or will it take wide-spread rioting that only serves to destroy lives and property in this country? Yes, it could happen, and the time may come sooner than later. But we must continue with hope and a caring spirit, to work hard and smart. Losing faith without "self-love" is a recipe for destruction of African-Americans in America. The "have-nots" cannot secure what the "haves" acquired over-time. The unequal distribution of wealth has always been in the society, but the lack of understanding that exists today is worthy of regularly reviewing the so-called biblical "caution meter."

CHAPTER FOUR

A RECIPE FOR HOPE AND UNDERSTANDING

G reetings everyone, what is in this so-called recipe for hope and understanding? Well, it includes finding the answers to the following questions with truth and knowledge. I have decided to list the entire issues at this point, where the reader may respond in his or her time frame. They are as follows and not necessarily in any order of importance.

1) Where is God?

2) Does He not care about all of His children? (African-Americans)

3) If so, why are they the underclass in America?

4) God heard the cries of those during biblical times, so why not today?

5) Are blacks not true believers?

6) Is He simply make-believe; and the former elders wanted to leave blacks with something to believe in based on their experiences, what they thought had happened?

7) Is God returning or coming back again?

8) Was He really on earth before?

9) Why does it happen that the rich seems to get richer? In contrast, the poor stays the same in most instances?

10) Are black sinners considered worse than those purported to have lived during biblical times?

11) How does one know when God forgives an individual?

12) Should blacks always have hope? And if so, when can they expect the deliverance to come, and by whom?

13) We have read articles regarding artificial intelligence (AI). Should blacks devote more time researching this phenomenon?

14) Where can black people find the answers to these and other questions?

15) Should there be an organized rally of blacks to ask God (if he exists, to come and help or aid them) with those solutions?

The previous questions would best be presented to those ministers of the gospel and not particularly for your expertise, although some readers may possess extensive knowledge in that profession. However, these are my perspectives on African-Americans, and their struggles, conflicts, and purposes in 21st century America. Most individuals in power refuse to speak frankly or candidly about those situations and provide realistic solutions. A significant number of the young African-Americans are uneducated, and those educated often find themselves in undereducated positions. That is because there are not enough available jobs to employ those needing to work. (See the previous chapter.) Are blacks to be considered lost or among the working poor? The majority of young males and particularly females have finished high school, and according to the latest statistics, a large percentage have completed at least two years of college or trade school. Excellent, but listening to the dominant race (white), one would not see those kinds of statistical results. What will it take to convince those without any skills and aptitudes to become productive citizens in the U.S.? Well, it is possible for them to become productive members of society with natural desires and aspirations, similar to those afforded by the majority of citizens in America? Or will they continue in the chaos of confusion, dismay, and poverty? There are chapters in the Bible that discuss how God challenged his people to believe and not quit or give up. I have often heard the cliché that, "good things come to those who wait, but not to those who wait too late!" An axiom that has been heard many, many times in the past. But African-Americans have heard similar sayings without results, time after time. Have they given up or stopped listening altogether? It is becoming more and more apparent that unless people possess some part of those listed values or should I say, "the so-called secular values of gold, silver, stocks, bonds, etc.," he or she will face severe hardships and poverty in America. Unfortunately, this author does not have solutions to the myriad of problems in America. If African-Americans are waiting for "God" to show them the way, then, it appears to me that there must be a change in their ways, replacing them with humility and love. However, I am not an official messenger of

God, as is proclaimed by many saints, prophets, apostles, ministers, soothsayers, etc.

Taste and see that the Lord is good; blessed is the man who takes refuge in him.

Psalm 34:8 (NIV)

CHAPTER FIVE

RELATED RESEARCH PERSPECTIVES

I recently recalled something from a book by the noted author, William J. Bennett (2013), former Secretary of Education during the years 1985-1988. The book was titled, *The Book of Man: Readings on the Path to Manhood*. What I recalled from the book was that it focused mainly on a cross-section of young men (Black, White, Asian, Mexican, etc.), who treated reading a book as the "plague." I recognize that getting children or young people to learn is difficult for many families whether they are attending middle, or high school. Furthermore, a significant amount of information obtained by Bennett was chosen to illustrate, verify, or inspire additional research and readings by the general public and researchers. That, I cannot stress enough because of the low reading levels of a vast number of children in this country. With the advent of computers, the internet, echoes, I Phones, and other electronic venues, reading printed books tend to be somewhat obsolete. Although his book is not focused on children or young adults per se, they find other activities to occupy their time, and reading books, magazines, periodicals, etc., does not fit with their lifestyle. That is an unfortunate occurrence for everyone since research suggests that America suffers (educationally), when reading or the lack thereof ceases to exist in a consistent manner. Just think, where will the future scientists scholars, poets, researchers, etc., emanate, if those kinds of activities continue to persist? The answer is to find ways to supplement reading technologically; but the major factor remains. That is, young African-Americans must understand, regardless of the mode or medium chosen, and just learn how to read, read, read, and read! I think it was Francis Bacon who postulated that "reading makes a full man," or something to it. Readers, what do you say?

Reading has always been stressed in the American educational system. The Bible was one of the first books that many African-Americans read or were taught to read. America is a Christian-based nation, as I have mentioned in a prior chapter, like it or not, that is a fact! Reading is a requirement when students are participating in those Christian –type activities. For a large number of Christians, black, white, and others, the Holy Bible forms the basis of their lives religiously, and everything thereof. It is coincidental that African-Americans of the past ages learned to read using that basic book. In the 21st century, a large majority of these youths do not read according to grade levels in formalized schools (most large urban public schools). It is not difficult to surmise one factor when determining why a large number of youths are resorting to violence of some kind, and particularly in many large urban cities. There is a large concentration of poverty, and they are residing therein. In contrast, I have mentioned several times in the book about the Bible and the part it played and continues to play in the lives of African-Americans. Now, I read a portion of this book titled, *Misquoting Jesus: the Story behind Who Changed the Bible and Why*, by Bart D. Ehrman (2005). My thoughts were that he would provide a clear and concise rendition, and how it changed his life from crime and poverty to hopes and beliefs. No, I was totally incorrect. It had nothing to do with my preconceived notions of what it contained. He provided readers with a profile of his life, beginning when he was wondering, as I, about his future and those difficult days of trials and tribulations. Ladies and gentlemen, I have never been so wrong in my many days on this earth. The man happened to be a college professor who had problems in his youth with what I would call, "finding God." I would not think that the common African-Americans would wonder each day of how and when they would or could find "God." He is considered to be with them daily, but not hearing their cries regarding improving their economic lives. Wow, how could we impose similar introspection toward African-Americans who are less educated, not with family members and do not consider their future as being important in the overall scheme of living, and development toward adulthood? If one was asked to answer the question of, "what would you consider as a recipe for life?" Would their answer surprise most questionnaires and fellow peers?

Live a life that reveals Godliness.

Or would the responses be, ---------"I do not expect to live beyond twenty-five years;" or "probably shot dead;" or "in an adult prison," or a "correction facility somewhere."

Many African-Americans simply finish high school, and attending a college is wishful thinking. They also tend not to find criticism with the Bible, but simply embrace the teachings of God and what has been passed on via elders and older family members. Why return to this example when there has been significant attempts to highlight minority killings? Ladies and gentlemen, I have made attempts to read and analyze those crime statistics the past six years, which have shown an increase in killings, and so-called racial hate crimes. Now while writing this afternoon, a similar headline sparked my attentive mechanism: "African -American killed by a policeman during routine traffic stop." This kind of view tends to make the newspaper headlines, but with cell phones, twitter and other media, it becomes quite attractive in our daily lives. In addition, media tends to thrive in reporting the negative about most events, and especially those involving African-Americans. What is the reason for otherwise not mentioning the event? Well, I cited one reason in a previous chapter. Another reason is that they serve to incite a few people. Readers, you may also be in a position to list those reasons similar and different from this author's.

A large percentage of young African-Americans, for which I am writing, tend not to finish high school, depending on the geographical areas cited, and many don't think of attending college. These young people, mostly males, have no future; at least, that is the consensus. Therefore, thinking beyond their environment is beyond their immediate comprehension. What they see and experience every day often becomes their lives. Mothers with children, many times without knowing the biological father of the child in question, are often unable to sustain their livelihood from infancy to adolescent. What kind of life can be expected by a society of kids from such up bringing? Can children be held accountable for their futures? Who should bear the burden or blame for whatever outcomes await the children in this country with that so-called ill-baggage? Who else should be held accountable for their results? My contention is that society cannot be expected to rear children in this country. The schools? No! Friends? No! Mothers and fathers? Finally, a yes! Whether you agree or disagree with my assessments of the matter, the parents are or should be held accountable! Those are personal accountability factors. Because each mother has a child, that becomes a personal choice to make, especially concerning when there is a new life. We (the public), cannot be held accountable for another individual's child, and the rearing thereof. That brings forth a personal issue to resolve. It becomes necessary for that person to be responsible for the life she or he brings into God's world or creation. Therefore, the result of what is being brought forth into this world has, and is becoming extremely disturbing. The reproduction of another has become more that a routine happening or course of action between men and women. The sad results of many pregnancies in this country are on television in the form of violence against each other, and society as a whole.

Readers, as I purported in a prior book, *The Journey of a Common Man: Perceptions and Reflections,* Johnson (2014), each baby born has a mother and father somewhere. They cry, wet, and most show emotions that kids make. What develops then become the issues? How, and when the social skills begin, and how, plus other environmental factors, tend to influence what kind of individual the child may develop and become in life. Yes, those are variables that cannot be predicted with a certain degree of accuracy. But studies have shown that an individual surrounded by harmful ills, and child-rearing skills, or lack thereof, may lead to dysfunctional results. These variables are conducive for a healthy and normal childhood. Most health officials conclude that there are fundamental facts regarding infants, which are consistent with many from birth to a certain age. For example, the length, weight, circumference, teeth, pubertal growth, and being aware of the consequences of their actions. The growing years---from infancy to adolescence, we see various feelings, problem behaviors in childhood and adolescent. They are probably due to a multiplicity of interacting factors. For example, the health, appearance, intelligence, entire personality of the child, and the relationship with all members of the family. The child's experiences at school, the neighborhood, including other rapid changes physically and sexually are noticeable. There is also a strong tendency to experiment. The conclusion appears to show that adjustment problems are with most young individuals from adolescent to young adulthood. Faced with the multifaceted array of challenges and situational concerns in the lives of these young people (18 to 30 years of age), the results may spell trouble for the general public. The community experiences of these young people may not be new, but what we see is a consistency toward deviant kinds of behavior and a troubling disregard for law and order in our society.

Readers, for experimental purposes, let us look at our youth, and a few of those factors listed by many health professionals and how they may impact individuals and their peers. I am not a clinical analyst or a trained psychiatrist. When an individual becomes a high school senior, the health and overall personal appearance has a large part to do with what is being tried out by him or her. Within the equation, his or her intelligence plays a significant role in what should be. The physical changes, which include those omnipresent sexuality factors, tend to dominate certain courses of action. For example, if young man A has a problem with many of those factors, and attends a predominately inner-city school, composed mostly of African-Americans, it is evident there are individuals who have little, if any, powerful positive home influence in his life. The results could be catastrophic! There could also be another factor called bullying, and that adds more so-called "fire" to the already unbalanced, what I call, "student equation." The oldest male in the family dwelling, without any male influence (no father, only a mother), who works occasionally, and on public assistance (welfare), is often the only common means of support for all. Gangs are quite prevalent in the neighborhood, and for several blacks, the temptation to become a member is often overbearing. A feeling of belonging is needed. A chance to satisfy the adolescence's need for immediate gratification, with practical items, has become extremely tempting to overlook. Well, the damage has been done; it is only a matter of time before his mother is among many of her peers, relatives, or parents, crying one night, learning that her baby has been shot and killed by neighborhood gang members. That is unfortunate, and the community vigils will be scheduled to highlight that violence should stop! Yeah! Sure! What about when he was bringing home the many hundreds of dollars weekly, saying that he was working at an unknown place or job? The mother could or should have inquired, but the damage had already been done, long, long ago. When? The change probably happened during early adolescent and perhaps even earlier. Many factors had already predicted his outcome. For example, the kind of school experiences, and the neighborhood, his physical and sexually changes, overall health, visual appearance, and his personality (which, if memory serves me accurately, is the total sum of an individual). Sad, sad, sad. Trying to contrast, compare and even relate those factors to many so-called middle-class whites, or African-Americans would be an injustice to them. Guns and other arms are readily available in many communities. There are many avenues for which they may be secured. It appears that many are available in certain African-American communities simply by inquiring and offering the amount of money needed to secure the purchase. Nowadays, they are available, in those areas, simply by asking on a street corner, neighborhood store, pool hall, etc. But most of those guns or weapons cannot be registered because they are secured illegally. The results, many innocent people are injured or killed by them for stupid reasons, for example, drugs, money, women, men and other kinds of illegal activities.

The most revealing part of my writings portrayed the subtle nature of how African-Americans have allowed the so-called dominant race (white) to dictate how they define themselves in most facets of human existence. For example, males, during slavery days viewed their sisters as queens, and for marriage, regardless of the color of their skin or pigmentation. However, after years and or should I say many, many, many decades of being subjugated by the masters, regarding racial matters, the guilt, that they were not superior as those of lighter color individuals, represented by the dominant race or slave owners, increased. The systems grew, hundreds and hundreds of years, and wealth added a very vital ingredient to what I call "racial education." Blacks were thought of, in many instances, to be less than animals that the master raised. Interracial sex, mostly without the permission of slave women, strengthened the race-color factor, particularly of males and their perspectives of women and their color. (Many knew the color situation that had permeated for centuries regarding racial color.) Light- skinned females and even males were considered to be superior in mind and body, compared to those who were of a darker-skin color. It was true then, and after hundreds of years, there continue to be vestiges of the same kind of color biases, not only by white, but many blacks.

In the 21st century, Americans are finally realizing that, and particularly blacks, the light –skinned females or males do not possess the so-called superior knowledge, and or skills. Those traits are based on the abilities of the individual, and not because of skin color. What took so long to see the change? Well, there is another point I also must reveal. This unexpected consequence has emerged. That is, many African-Americans have moved from dating light-skinned blacks to dating whites and those of Mexican/Hispanic descent. No, it is not the appropriate time for a discussion on what I call non-sense matters. But it is quite interesting! Many years have passed from the introduction of African-Americans into this country as slaves, to the present 21st century. True, there have been incredible gains to the present. However, what prevails is this kind of "everything is alright" aura, and "you are doing very well as a people," and "you are equal to us (dominant race)," syndromes. Well, most realize that it is a common misnomer. With all of the class "hyperbole about race," the issues continue to prevail. I ask anyone to visit a major urban city in this country. After visiting, could or would the individual or person answer only one question, truthfully? The question: "If you were to divide that city into only two sections, which part would be considered one where the dominant race lives, versus the area that houses the other (non-dominant class)? I do not enjoy revealing that kind of national information in this book. We all acknowledge, but will not admit, regardless of the reason(s). Now, again, why are many young black males resorting to the streets saying that particular white law enforcement people are killing blacks, and often without provocation? Readers, we know that not all males, and now females, are adhering to the requests made by some law enforcement officers. They are simply giving them a reason to finally go on a "Kill a Nigger Patrol," legally! Yes, I used the (N) word term, something that African-Americans use toward each other on a daily basis. The law enforcers should not be killing individuals unless they are provoked or it is a matter of life and death. That is a very delicate situation because, as has been said publicly, those officers are "afraid" in many, many situations. Can African-Americans just do what is asked by the law enforcement officers? Neither wants to die for the most part. But if someone looks for a reason to shoot, during those stops, as an officer, in most instances, one can be found. Why give him or her reason? It takes a well-disciplined man or woman to maintain common sense, and professionalism, in those kinds of matters. Let no one say that he or she would view it in another way, unless in that particular situation, at that moment! Then, the results may be quite unusual, if recorded.

I have taken many directions in this book thus far, with very few, if any given suggestions for solving the race dilemma in America. The primary focus of the first book was not to offer solutions to what has been a boiling racial situation for hundreds of years. Why has the matter not been resolved long before the 21st century? One reason could be that those individuals of the dominant race in power refuse to openly debate and discuss the matter to bring forth an amicable solution. There are over 300 million inhabitants in this country, and what an excellent time to begin the dialogue!

The electing of a President (so-called African-American),

in 2008, and re-elected in 2012, has failed to produce changes necessary for a solution. Yes, he was of colors, whose mother and grandmother were both Caucasians, and reared in the fiftieth state of the union, Hawaii. He was to provide African-Americans with hope, but failed to deliver. The African-American community made a painful mistake by assuming that he knew what they needed, or desired from him, as president. Sorry! Mr. Author, what should be done by African Americans? First, I will address an area that should be familiar to all readers. Alright, excellent, you may have guessed. God. I know that does not fit with many people in American, although America is a so-called Christian country. Those with continued beliefs in God can relate. However, those who are not, may have heard of God and his teachings, but might have chosen to try or not engage therein.

History has provided us with many versions of the Bible and with numerous translations. I have cited or made reference to the same in my earlier chapters. Most protestants adopted the King James Version of the Holy Bible. Whereas, Catholics are Christians, but use what they call the Catholic Bible. Most ministers who have ever attended a seminary, synagogue, etc., or a school for religious training, have studied the history of religion. Many decide to omit those kinds of teachings to their congregations once they leave those institutions and begin their ministries. Why? One possibility could be that they want to have and maintain a group attending the church that provides financial support on a regular basis. Introducing controversial spiritual nature to congregations where the masses are high school grads at best, would be asking for a failed ministry. Therefore, many take the literal Bible translations and convey those kinds of stories and applications to illustrate their positions. In essence, convey meanings where the masses will understand and accept; thereby, ensuring the continued survival for years and beyond.

A large number of African-Americans continue to praise and serve the almighty God. That is mostly a tradition passed down by their elders, and through the hundreds of years. I will not provide a historical knowledge from whence Christianity started in this country; mostly it was long before slavery, but in many parts of America, the traditions and practices of old traditional religious-based God acts continue. However, from my current readings on Christianity and religious practices of African-Americans, a significant number of young adults have abandoned the practice of attending church, as was done for years and years before the

21st century. The practice of not attending church is particularly common amongst young black males, and the overall male population of Americans. (I envisioned that in many sections of the traditional practices are more widespread than others.) (For example, the Southern States, when compared to the Western States.) A few Southern states are, MS, AL, GA, TN, etc., versus Western States as, CA, OR, MN, etc., to name a few.

In years past, for example, 50-100 years ago, churches were meeting places for African-Americans, and young people were able to find mates of similar ages and personal attractions. The 21st century offers significantly different avenues to meet and greet each other and find friends. However, with increased communicative avenues, chances are also conducive for foul play and other kinds of evil situations. Nowadays, this kind of evil practices happens more frequently than not. An increase in crimes and other criminal activities often follows those new forms of communications. Thus, sophisticated features also attract evil cultures, regardless of the skin color. With those new devices, expensive costs are associated therewith. But many cannot afford the new and or technology kind of devices, and temptation begins to make people uneasy and violence and other unsafe practices tend to follow. Our world seems to be getting more violent each day, but can we use the excuse of stories and or tales found in the Holy Bible to justify those deeds?

If memory serves me correctly, my research shows that King VI of Scotland and King James I of England played a significant part in what is read today. However, there has been little attention or anything else devoted to his character and rulings as a king. It's hard to discuss subjects of their relevant context without providing some evidence for writings or epitaph drawings or any kinds of communication during those centuries. From my research, it appeared that King James VI of Scotland and King James I of England was one in the same. Yes, he was King James VI of Scotland and in1603, became King of England, and his title for that became King James I of England (McElwee (1974). This was evident during the seventeenth and sixteenth centuries. But how does this have any relationship to African-Americans and their plight in the 21st century? Writers of that time choose not to engage into the character and reputation of those kinds of men. They could and did as they pleased with little government interference. African-Americans did not or have not enjoyed those kinds of privileges during most of their lives. As I have stated in a prior chapter, they were bound by what the dominant race dictated and how they should respond according. This started with slavery incidents and has continued until the 21 century, although there have been significant advances by them. However, with the wave of crimes throughout this country, it appears that the concentration, once again, is on the incarceration and subjugation thereof. Because the African-American communities are first in unemployment, first in crimes against each other, and first in low earning wages, the temptation of significant crimes increase, without any legitimate means of escape For years, African-American communities have believed that God would supply them with all of their needs, if only there was a trust factor; and "not give-up." For instance, "He will not fail you." Well, in the 21st century, many tend not to believe those sayings anymore. Many conclude that they are simply "Bible Tales" to keep everyone in their proper places, ----and that is "not to challenge the dominant race" (Caucasian). I will not return to the old slavery kind of mentality that was taught and learned years ago. The 21st century has brought forth new concerns, but based on an old theme. That is, the African-Americans place in America, and what should be done to maximize their potential?

CHAPTER SIX

FACE THE FACTS

T he challenge for African Americans is to debunk the adage of not being interested in the future, low self- esteem, crime oriented, killing of each other, and not being worthy of a prosperous and beneficial life, versus an actual return to the idea of family. There is a genuine need for them to show the love of life, and particularly one's own, with the need to express emotional understanding about people and diversity issues. They also need to stop allowing the dominant race to control and dictate what should, and what they would be, based on their knowledge of the issues, and the minorities. How can the dominant race articulate the way a particular group of people should respond to issues they created, and are intimating, based on the idea of them? Blacks have been dealing with subjugation issues orchestrated by the dominant race for hundreds of years. And quietly, the dominant race has launched another effort to restrict what they had been trying or doing for centuries. Has it worked? Certainly! But the time has finally evolved to eradicate those kinds of personal tactics, and look at people (blacks) for who they are. That is, intelligent, God-fearing, aggressive- thinking beings who just happened to be of another color (pigmentation). These are the same people who they so-labeled in past generations as being lazy, non-productive, dumb, and only athletic (who commanded millions of dollars, with limited and less than average intelligence). Most African-Americans are ambitious young men and women who also deserve a place in this world, and that is, the same as the dominant race of people. For years, the saying was that "How can they learn when the emphasis is not on anything of value?" Sorry dominant race, a change has happened, and it is coming your way soon. Blacks can and have become whatever their interest shows, with perseverance, hard work and a desire to achieve. There is only one way to go, which is higher and up higher, reaching whatever endeavors are available.

My book, in contrast to the one written by Kelley B. Douglas (2015), *Stand your Ground: Black Bodies and the Justice of God*, is an attempt to provide personal in-depth views regarding African Americans, and the divisiveness that rest therein. Also, how the so-called "have- nots" often dominate the negative perceptions labeled given to all. Historically, African-Americans have always been the second- class citizens because of the laws, rules, regulations, and overall prejudice views of the dominant race toward them. Hundreds of years have passed since they first arrived in America; but have they quit striving for better opportunities? No, I do not think that they have given-up. If their communities would only reflect, if possible, how conditions were during the past hundreds of years, a rude awakening would happen. They are present in the 21st century because of the diligence and perseverance of their ancestors, years, and years before today.

If memory serves me correctly, in 2014, records indicated that there were over one million African-Americans in the higher education systems in this country. Those records did not include GED, skills, and or trade institution programs. Is this a step in the right direction to rid individuals from mediocre to possible higher paying jobs, and improved standards of living in America? I think so! All educational improvements will be needed to survive and exist, during the 21st century and beyond. We learn from those numbers that it will take a plethora of people to fill all of

the jobs for the next generation. The kind and type will alter, but

opportunities will be there if one has the skills needed to master

the requirements and job functions. Might I remind all blacks,

that it was President Lyndon B. Johnson, from Texas, who was

not received very well by African-Americans, even though he

was a Democrat and President J. Kennedy's vice-president. Also,

I can recall that they did not trust a southerner, from which

Johnson was of that background. Later during the continuation

of Kennedy's term, and subsequent elections to the Presidency,

he tried desperately to pass legislation to erase discrimination

and racial hatred. According to the Department of Education,

National Center for Educational Statistics (2000-10), the slogan

used in 1965 by President L.B.J., to identify his legislative program

of national reform was the "Great Society." That included what

was known as, "war on poverty," and "federal support for

education, medical care for the elderly, and legal protection for

blacks, deprived of voting rights by state regulations." (Dept. of

Education, National Center for Educational Statistics (2000-

10). He also proposed a new department of housing and urban

development to utilize housing projects. Surprisingly, congress enacted almost all programs, which turned out to be the largest number of such measures since the "new deal."

In contrast, ladies and gentlemen, most or well over 50 percent of black voters in the past 2008 and 2012 elections supported Mr. Obama. Not to sound jealous, or mean-spirited, but what kind of proposals have come from his eight years in office, other than the controversial so-called Obama Care Health Plan! None that may have specifically assisted blacks and other minorities with struggles in education and particularly the poverty they claim existed in America. Yes, things were different fifty-one years ago, but African-Americans did not overwhelmingly vote for or elect L.B.J. as they did with Mr. Obama. In addition, compared to the support he received versus approximately 25 percent for Johnson, there should have been more programs proposed and legislations for African-Americans. But where are they? I will not say anything else about that topic; rather, readers may draw their conclusions.

To demonstrate my equality of thinking, memory has that there were many programs proposed by Presidents in America. But may I cite the following proposed and enacted during the presidency of Mr. Franklin D. Roosevelt? I will. Most of his programs were to assist people of the U.S. business or government. For example, The

Emergency Banking Act/Federal Deposit Insurance Corporation (FDIC), Federal Energy Relief Administration (FERA), Civil Works Administration and National Instructional Recovery Act (NIRA). Two others were widely known and are poplar today: The Tennessee Valley Authority (TVA) and the Social Security Administration. (Department of Education. National Center for Educational Statistics (2000-10). Roosevelt, according to my recollection, was the 32nd president of the U.S. (1933-1945). He was credited with guiding America through World War II. Most of the programs he proposed are in existence today. Simply remarkable! How have they survived this many years? It was through, hard work and an expression of understanding to the overall nature of being a President.

In the words of Colin Powell, former Chairman of the U.S. Joint Chiefs of Staff (1989-93), "There is no secret to success. It is the result of perfection, hard work, learning from failure, loyalty, and persistence." I am also captivated by another one of his quotes. That is, "If you are going to achieve excellence in big things, you develop the habit in little matters." "Excellence is not an exception; it is a prevailing attitude." Powell (2003). My only comment was: "Where was I when that man voiced those words or comments?"

Many blacks or minorities in the country were not well-read, but Colin Powell was not in a major U.S. position when he spoke those phrases. It is inspiring to know of, and to have read, that there are blacks who have made significant strides to greatness despite the racial and subjugated or prejudicial setbacks, all resulting from racism in America.

Another perspective regarding racism in America and it's affect in the African-American communities, tends to be in some aspects, "contentment," with what has been in their lives if it satisfied their present situation. In essence, people do not change drastically! That is certainly applicable when referring to the Federal U.S. Government. Many elected lawmakers tend to reject, in many instances, comments or suggestions that could make a difference in the lives of most Americans, particularly blacks and other minorities. But in many cases, they make excuses; find reasons for what could be considered the so-called, "status quo." No wonder Americans continue to be stuck in monetary debt. Also, those rich or as I refer to them as, "haves," do not allow the majority of "have-nots" to make strides toward encroachment on their powers of "richness." Most Americans can't understand the rules and regulations that govern monetary funds. Many of the lawmakers cannot either. They employ or must rely upon the services of professional CPA'S, planners, bankers, etc., to make solid financial decisions. Meanwhile, the country continues in massive outbursts of crime, particularly in the major urban cities, where there are large percentages of minorities (Blacks and Hispanics). To justify what I have just cited, according to a report by Michael B. Sauté, Douglass A. McIntyre, Ashley C. Allen, Alexander E.M. Hess, Lisa Nelson, and Sivan, in Yahoo.com; "The Most Dangerous cities in America, 2012 Wall Street Review of 2011, and FBI Crime data," showed that violent crime rose in most states in this country. "In seven of the ten cities, murder rates increased 10% and up." "The top 5 cities making the list were: 5-Memphis, TN; 4-Oakland, CA; 3-St. Louis, MO; 2-Detroit, MI; and 1-Flint, MI." Among those cities tested, I found a factor that is appalling. The unemployment rates were over 11% for each city. However, in recent years, 2016 to be exact, "most crime rates have fallen to one/ half of what they were, from the initial rates of Memphis, TN – 11%; Oakland, CA –15%, St. Louis, MO-11%, Detroit, MI -19% and Flint, MI 18%." Most cities mentioned have a predominant of African- Americans and other minorities living in those areas.

Help is often a prelude to success.

Previously, I had addressed the African Americans and their so-called religious faith. What tends to be troubling during the 21st century is a breakdown in morals, values, character, self-understanding, and demonstrating the differences between right and wrong, or good and evil. Also, those who are between the ages (18-30) years are in a dilemma. Comments often heard are, "Should we take what ought to be ours or wait until society decides what it is or should be?" Fascinating! This writer is an old senior man (over 70 years of age). He was involved in all kinds of subjugated racial practices. His observations of why young blacks are having a few problems-in-living are two-fold: First, they are in time-changing environments that stress "materialistic" visual items. And second, that the older generation of African-Americans who were grandparents and great-grandparents, are mostly gone (deceased), and if not, are significantly impaired physically and or mentally. They possessed the understanding that should have been treasured and retained by their off-springs and beyond. But society changed, and they were not prepared to make adjustments which affected their lives. Thereby, 21st century young black mothers, and others, are having a tough time in the "child-rearing business." The difficulties become apparent when the gap in household salaries is revealed. The differences connote that the classification cited is that there are the "haves" and "have-nots." They are also greatly divided. According to news report from networks such as CNN, Fox, MSNBC, etc., the "haves" are even richer, while the "have-nots," are significantly lower on the materialistic scale.

Readers, I have cited effects of religion as it related to African -Americans, and their continued struggles in America, racism as it affects the same, and how the dominant race reacts when rights are involved. However, I have not investigated those entities in-depth because it would require that readers scan more pages than actually reading them. The summary would begin, and it would not be appropriate for me to provide discussions regarding those areas not fully explained in the fore stated, but mentioned.

As a closing observation from this author, somehow, "we need to help make this world a better place to live."

CHAPTER SEVEN

PERSONAL PERSPECTIVES

The final segment of this book relates a more positive aspect of African-Americans and other minorities living in America. I noticed an article in the Washington Post by Ben Guarino, March 14, 2017, that I thought was "disturbing," but true. Two of the statements are as follows: "People often see black men larger and stronger than white men, even when they're not." "Even if white and black men are the same heights and weights, people tend to perceive black men as taller, more muscular and heavier." Furthermore, this was in a "Psychological Survey, published in the American Psychological Association's Journal of Personality and Social Psychology, "exploring stereotypes about perceptions of male bodies." The author also states the study found that, "Non-black participants believed black men to be more capable of physical harm than white men of the same size." The results also suggested that "non-black observers thought that police would be more justified to use force on these black men, even if they were unarmed as opposed to their white male counterparts." Guarino (2017). Hello America, that is my point in this book, summarized by scholars and acted out by society in the 21st century. In essence, white men see black men differently from themselves, as was previously summarized. Yes, I could also have another chapter written about the prior information cited in that survey. America continues to be a racist nation, whether the political leaders want to admit it or not. You may now draw your own conclusions. Good luck!

According to the U.S. Government Statistics (2014), there are over one million African-Americans enrolled in some form of higher education (which included college or university or paraprofessional, trade and other kinds of schools). What can we assume by such numbers and or percentages of the young black ages 18-30? I will relate one important point for discussion. According to the same statistics, the number and percentage of blacks 25 and over, with a high school diploma or greater in 2014, was 19.7 percent. Whereas, the number of blacks enrolled in undergraduate colleges in 2014, compared to 2009, showed an increase of 5.3 percent. In the year 2000, yes, there were more male blacks in prison or jail than enrolled in postsecondary education. Those numbers have reversed. How have we seen a change in the numbers? Why? Yes, as of 2010, there were approximately 844,600 in prison or jail. In contrast, during the next year, over 1,341,354 were enrolled in postsecondary education. What a remarkable turnaround.

I have alluded to the facts earlier in my writings that police killing of African-Americans has attracted significant attention during the past two or three years. However, there have always been many citizens killed by law enforcement officers yearly, and the numbers have increased with protests. For the record, white American people are shot by police and killed at higher numbers, according to the Washington Post. However, "Blacks, account for 24 percent of those fatally shot and killed by the police, despite being just 13 percent of the U.S. population." That means, "Blacks are 2.5 times more likely than white Americans to be shot and killed by police officers." Washington Post (2017). It also displays a chart (not included) that shows some lower crime cities with high police shootings and "vice versa," according to Snopes.com: "In America, regarding white police shootings, there are larger numbers than blacks, but overall whites are statistically less likely to be killed by police than blacks." Allen, Hess, McIntyre, Nelson, Saute and Sivan (2012). Readers, therein lay the problem or dilemma. With that being a fact, should the black community assume and or conclude that the law enforcement officers are often prejudicial against them and or show racism in dealing with the same and other minorities they stop, regardless of the reason(s)? Readers, you may draw your conclusions based on the facts previously cited. But, can the issues be solved by the continuation of past practices or impressions and stereotypes about certain racial groups and or minorities? Personally, I do not think that is an active position. Both the Africans-Americans and law enforcements throughout the U.S. and other minorities, must begin to understand each other, and try eliminating or dismissing pre-judged opinions about each other. Invariably, those kinds of issues and behaviors affect individuals and can carry on into day-to-day actions, especially on-the-job performances.

Well, as I sit at my desk reviewing the prior night's victory for Mr. Donald Trump over Ms. Hillary Clinton, a CNN commentator implied that, "a white man was using words about a country in need of a change." He was absolutely correct, even though there was no explanation. The dominant race seems to or encountered enough of 8 years commanded by a so-called African-American President. He did not adhere to the label of the "African-American" racial code, given to him by the ruling establishment. Yes, they had enough, eight years (Democrats), an African-American President, elected years ago, amidst the worse financial collapse in America, since the depression of the 1920s. I contend that the main ingredient which caused the historic change in presidents was "money," or "the lost thereof." When the dominant race saw that so-called previously cash commodity lost, whatever was necessary to recover the same was on the table. That meant electing a so-called president (a man of so-called color), Mr. B. Obama. He did manage to energize the country, and the majority of women, to the slogans of "yes, we can," and "change." Today, the country has also signaled another change was needed; and will be coming. What kind and when? Well, as I write February 09, 2017, since the inauguration, Mr. Trump has brought forth a so-called change in how Washington, D.C. politics has been run and operated for years. That is what he campaigned for, and practically tried to implement during the first few months in office. My comment is: "It is too early for me to be objective in an assessment of the new President. But time will answer all questions."

Be on your guard; stand firm in the faith; be men of courage; be strong.

I Corinthians 16:13 (NIV)

In fairness, Democrats, "the fight was long and fierce." Your past President did not do enough to ensure a victory. Personally, I do not think he really wanted Ms. Clinton to win! Okay, some readers will say "boo" to me, but I will say to you, "Prove me wrong?" You cannot! Most African-Americans did not vote, and half of those who did, chose another candidate. What caused this to transpire, since four and eight years prior, Mr. Obama had carried the same, and a few whites, especially women? I will tell you, "The African-American voters were tired of the President." Yes, I made that statement. For eight years, what happened to those promises made? The main group that assured his victory in both elections was not pleased with his prior performances. Therefore, trying to energize them again was not going to work. In essence, "You fooled us once, shame on us; fooled us twice, shame on you;

and trying to fool us the third time, not going to happen!" And it didn't; Ms. Clinton lost the election! End of story.

I remember what Mr. Trump said during his campaign: "We will take back America." Translation: We will make America white again! Many African-Americans will not agree, but it does not matter, the deed has been done, in spite of Ms. Clinton receiving a significantly larger number of the popular votes count. This writer is not angry or disappointed with the 2016 Presidential election results. Just as when the former President, Mr. George Bush, was in control, and we experienced the greatest economic "meltdown" since the great depression of the twenties, thus, bring forth the first president of color, Mr. Obama. He is therefore the recipient of being the one who ignited the "return to America," chant of Mr. Trump. Using another phrase of many elderly or African American women, "What goes around comes around." And as I have cited previously, America was also not ready for a female president. Sorry, some of my readers, but that is true; if not, she would have won handily. It was not to be, and did not occur. America was not ready for another historical occurrence that had happened when Mr. Obama was elected in 2008, and re-elected President in 2012. Americans went with a controversial white male, not entirely endorsed by the party he represented, Republicans. Just think, "To elect a woman in America as the first female President?" I do not think so! Readers, simply think of the many men who have tried and failed at the presidency, and to have the first female or woman in American history become the President of America in 2017? The country was not, and is not ready for that drastic change, having been through one just eight years ago. It was not going to happen! The dominant race was elated that they finally, so-called, "regained America," and to never again prevent that phenomenon from re-occurring.

Whatever many people have said about Mr. Trump, it matters not, because he is in the White House for at least four years, unless impeachment or an unfortunate situationoccurs to interrupt that stay. I envision that if he remains for the four years term, significant changes in what has prevailed in the nation's capital via political dealings will also be made. Remember readers, I have reminded Americans that "change" is difficult for all to feel comfortable with, and challenging for us to like, and make adjustments. We enjoy the "status quo." No, I do not agree with many of Mr. Trump's propositions, but my contentions were similar toward the previous President, Mr. Obama. However, there are a few that have my support. I am encouraged to take, and as I previously stated, "A wait and see," approach before "ringing the final bell," regarding him, because "it may toll for thee!" As a God-fearing person, may he find peace during his presidency, and "somehow seek the guidance and direction from the Almighty God, always."

CHAPTER EIGHT

SUMMARY

P erhaps, the African American community will use the Trump Presidency to rally around the man and seek higher standards in education, and housing, to try and stop crime, violence against each, and toward all races, including the law enforcement personnel. No, it is not a difficult feat to accomplish. It does not take marching, candle burning, etc., to affect changes. It is simply to show a little common sense, a positive mind-set, and love of self, along with extending that love to each other. A helping hand is better than a bullet to the heart. Blacks must let the President know that their communities are also tired of the same thing over and over, that other administrations have said. That would be, promises, promises, promises, not reinforced by actions. Yes, they are tired of low standards associated with schools and education, crime-riddled communities, substandard housing, the killing of youths, adults, each other, and drugs, drugs, and more drugs, which are destroying families and communities. Yes, African-Americans are ready to change and seek assistance from those willing to invest in the future of all Americans with those issues. They are prepared to build the new and renovate the old, when and where necessary. They seek a "helping hand," not a "giving hand." There is the future, and of their communities and America. Come; "let us work together, Mr. President." They are ready and hope you are also willing to help them drive out the criminals, convicted felons, and drugs from their communities, where hard-working, honest and God loving people are waiting and eager to begin a new journey. Can they count on you? Yes, I think so!

Ladies and gentlemen, I dare not leave you with despair and a lack of hope regarding the future of America and everyone therein. So much has been written, stated, and analyzed about race, prejudice, and religion as it relates to the current state of affairs in this country. Many writers, both historians, and legal scholars have proposed solutions to all of the aforesaid. However, the problems continue to exist. Yes, they do! My solutions cannot solve the problems either. So, why write about those solutions being proposed and implemented without results? Many writers are taking either a scholarly, historical and or political model to resolve what has and is systemic in nature.

Rejoice and be glad, for your reward is great in heaven.

Matthew 5:12 (RSV)

The problems have existed for hundreds of years, only to linger and linger, and linger in the minds of those living in America. Are we fooling ourselves by failing to face facts that have been around for ages? I think so! Please pardon my analogy, but if one sees a purple cow and a so-called green camel, what say you? Call the cow purple and move on. Why analyze being called that which is not? In essence, everyone is different, everyone! Sisters, brothers, etc., all are different. The problem therein rests with those drawing the conclusions and making the different paradigms. Just call or addressing the situation as it is, and moving one, should be the primary purpose. Is that difficult? I think not! The diversity in America and even the world is excellent, and should be, in many instances applauded for people being innovative and new, versus the same. Without diversity of individuals, what would happen? I think it would be boring and non-productive living. There would not be doctors, pilots, engineers, military people, poets, musicians, scholars, and law enforcement personnel, etc.; you got the picture without an exhaustive listing of professions. Individuals are learning and must continue learning to make adjustments in their lives regarding people, places, and things. Whether they like or dislike a person, situation, or another variable, which is not in the equation, the world's existence is at stake. For African-Americans, the time has come for togetherness again! That is a statement of, "all for one and one for all." It has been an old sports adage regarding how a team must or should play. In life, as a common poor man, I am inclined to agree with the idea.

People have begun moving away from the so-called "bad areas," but the uneducated and less-affluent African Americans and others have stayed. Why? These reasons have been well-chronicled by others and the mass media. Economically, many blacks have moved up and away for the areas called "ghetto." The media and other blacks say that they are poor and cannot do any better. Yes, that may be correct in many instances, but what say you to when most of those in the ghettos have the latest new cell phones, video games, tennis (shoes), sports regalia, hair accessories, and other materialistic items? However, when asked, "How are the children, their grades and progress in school? One may receive mixed responses. For example, "They are doing okay," "He or she could do better," or "I don't have enough to pay for the field trip to see a new movie that is now showing at "Blue Cat Cinema." My contention is that "yes," they may be living in "poverty," but I call it "Prioritized Poverty." The term can be loosely defined as "items of non-value, which cannot lead to a child's or children success." Mothers and fathers, what about investing in an internet connection, computer, tutoring, or after-school grade improvement sessions, and the likes? But no, one only hears about the poverty that exists in those areas as if they prevent realistic learning from taking place. Tragic!!! They are excuses, excuses, excuses, excuses. That is not the case, readers. Prioritize what is important and ensure the same. All poverty does not equate to non-success, it may impede the progress, but there are ways to achieve, in spite of the many ill obstacles. I challenge you to make the sacrifices and using a famous slogan, "just succeed." The African-American communities must demonstrate to those in political power that they are people to be "reckoned with." But the major part is that they should begin to show respect for each other, and thereby demonstrate love, and caring for the same. Jobs and the development thereof through technology and educational opportunities must be at the forefront. Yes, there will always be the 5 or 10 percent of a population that will continue in their wayward ways (drug, prostitution, gang, in essence, crime), but the non-criminals must pave the way for all African-Americans and stop or stamp-out the wave of criminals and their activities. If not, it threatens to ruin them and the progress that has been made toward equality. I have stopped short of making any drastic proposals in order to alleviate crime in those communities and other areas. However, I did not mention precisely who is responsible for the crimes in those communities. Now, I will make my controversial opinions regarding what could be or tried to minimize violence in those crime-infested areas. First, who are the chief proponents of crime in those areas? A rather complex answer, but for the most part, they are criminals from repeat performances, and those newly ordained or with criminal-related contacts. And second, what can be done with those in prison with simply drug-related offences? Well, the criminal justice system needs to be retooled with innovative approaches to the same old drug-related situations. Those problems tend to foster killings and other serious crimes. If an individual that is convicted of a drug-related minor crime, (just selling and other kinds of distribution-related situations), the chances of he or she ever securing a legitimate job or employment once released is almost impossible. However, if there were programs, whereas their records would be expunged after being successful in certain government jobs, rebuilding the infrastructure, and other kinds of positions for a certain period of time, without any altercations or trouble, the records would be cancelled. However, if they chose not to accept a position or returned to a life of crime, minor or serious, they would be returned to jail or prison for a mandatory sentence of 10 years, without the possibility of parole. This is only a possibility to be researched and maybe, implemented. Mind you, ordinary non-criminal citizens would receive first choice for those jobs. After all had been filled with non-criminal individuals, the remainder would somehow be available for those who were recently released and could not find or accept jobs in the public sector, because most jobs do not prefer individuals with criminal records. Nothing else is working, because they cannot get a job after prison and without funds, they will reenter the life of crime to make monies for their survival. I am not a philosopher, but only an utterly ordinary man with an optimistic concept of living. That allows me to make uncommon remarks, and sometimes introduce controversial rhetoric, and suggestions, regarding living in America and the global society.

BIBLIOGRAPHY

American Psychological Association's Journal of Personality, "Exploring Stereotypes About Perceptions of Male Bodies," Monday, Psychological Survey, APA, Washington, D.C., 2017.

American Psychological Association's Journal of Personality and social psychology, "Exploring Stereotypes about Perceptions of Male Bodies," Washington, D.C., 2017.

BJS, National Prisoner Statistic Program, Federal Justice Statistics Program, National Corrections Reporting Program (NCRP), 2015-2019 Cooperative Agreement. Survey Of Inmates in State and Local Correctional Facilities, and National Inmate Survey 2010.

Bennett, William J., Secretary of Education (1985-1988), "The Book of Man: ReadingsOn the Path to Manhood," Nashville, TN: Nelson Books and Thomas Nelson, Inc., 2013.

Brown, Douglas K., "Stand your Ground: Black Bodies and the Justice of God." Orbis Books, Mary Knoll, New York, N.Y., 2015.

Clarion-Ledger, "B. Obama Era: Have Race Relations Changed in the U.S. under the First Black President?" Associated Press, Jackson, MS, 2012.

Department of Education. National Center for Education Statistics, Integrated Postsecondary Education System, Enrollment Survey, 2000-10. Institute of Education Sciences, Potomac Center Plaza, Washington, D.C., USA.

Ehrman, Bart D., Misquoting Jesus: The Story Behind Who Changed the Bible and Why, New York: Harper Collins Pub., New York, 2005.

Fraser, Antonia, King James, VI of Scotland, I of England, London: Weidenfeld & Nicolson, 1994.

From Wikipedia, the free encyclopedia (Redirected from James of England). Britannica Together. "About King James I of England of Holy Bible, January, 2001.

Johnson, C. Samuel, II, "The Journey of a Common Man: Perceptions and Reflections," Denver, CO., Outskirts Press, Inc., 2014, Cover Photo by photographer Kai Productions/ Reel Walk Cinema, L.L.C.

Keeanga-Yamahtta Taylor, "Black Lives Matter to Liberation." Chicago, IL, Haymarket Books, 2016.

KJV, King James Version of the Bible, 1611.

Lenning, O.T.Variable Selection and Measurement Careers. In E. Pascerella (Ed.), New Directions for Institutional Research: Studying student Attrition (35-54). San Francisco: Jossey-Bass., 1982.

McElwee, William L., The Wisest Fool in Christendom; the reign of King James I and Westport, Conn., Greenwood Press, 1994,

Merriam-Webster Dictionary, Fifth Edition, Springfield, MA.; Houghton Miffin Miffin, 2016.

National Center for Education Statistics, Institute of Education Sciences, Washington, D.C., 550 12th St. SW, 2014.

NIV, New International Version of the Bible, 2011.

Obama, Barach, Speech delivered in Philadelphia, PA, 5-08-2008, Transcript in the New York Times://nytimes.com/2008/03/18us/politics/18 text-Obama,html

Pew Research Center, hhp://www.pewresearch.org/fact-tank/2016/07/08/how-americans-view-the-black-lives-mattermovement.

Powell, Colin L., U.S. Secretary of State, Jan. 20, 2001-Nov., 2004), New York: "A Collection of Personal Quotes," 2003.

The American Heritage, "The New Dictionary of Cultural Literacy, third ed., Houghton Miffin Co., Springfield, MA; 2005.

"The Most Dangerous Cities in America, 2012, "24/7 Wall Street, Review of 2011 FBI Crime Date," Yahoo.com. Michael B.Saute, Douglass A McIntyre, Ashley C. Allen, Alexander E. M. Hess, Lisa Nelson and Sivan.

The Mother and Child Health and Education Trust a U. S. @ non profit organization our Portals and sites, 2017.

The Washington Post, Ben Guarino, Brauchli, Marcus, Editor, Washington, D.C., 3/14/ 2017.

REV, Revised English Version of the Bible, 1901.

RSV, Revised Standard Version of the King James Bible, 1901.

U. S. Census Bureau 201, U.S. Government Statistics Washington, D.C., 2010.

Winfrey, Oprah, "The Life You Want," Flatiron Books, a division of Macmillan U.S. Pub, 2017.